AF492216

Which We Is Me?

Poems from the Guild Caretaker,
Nicholas "Cobalt Hearth" LaHusen

Copyright © 2026 Pantheon Arts Community Storytelling
Forward and After Thoughts copyright © 2026 by Nicholas Lahusen

The scanning, uploading, and distribution of this book without permission is a theft of the author's intellectual property. If you would like permission to use material from the book (other than for review purposes), please contact communitystudio@pantheonarts.org. Thank you for your support of the author's rights.

All rights reserved under International and
Pan-American Copyright Conventions.
Published in the United States by Pantheon Arts PDX's imprint
The Ephemeral Aperture in Portland, Oregon.
Distribution through IngramSpark

Pantheon Arts Community Storytelling
The Ephemeral Aperture
Portland, Oregon
pantheonarts.org

Which We is Me? / by Nicholas "Cobalt Hearth" LaHusen - 1st ed.
ISBN 979-8-9930484-6-8
1. Poetry (Poetic Works By One Author) 2. Mental Health
Published May 25, 2026.

Interior Layout Design by Kat Cramer
Interior Layout Design Assistance by Giacomo Reineri
Book Cover Illustrated by Alex Greene
Cover © 2026 Pantheon Arts Community Storytelling

Agonizing Consonance Honorable Mention:
Chronic Pain Project

Foreword & Dedications

The sections of the book follow part of a personal journey through the other side of a healed and healing psyche by Nicholas LaHusen, but this book is not meant to be about them in its entirety; which is why the "Cobalt Hearth" is the name on the front page.

It is a chosen name meant to strike a flame of hope within yourself; because you are not alone, and when you sit around this fire sparked from lights within each becomes able to share truths that were hidden - even those one hides from themselves.

To those versions of us that were lost for us to be here now - thank you for helping us to witness this self, ever-growing to an ideal self, and be able to share it proudly.

Thank you to that one above all that gave me solace and hope in a time when I was adrift with neither. I know that I could not be the person I am today without the love that has been given to me by them.

Thank you for helping me to heal beyond the scapes that I thought impossible to cross, for giving me the courage to push myself beyond comfort and into that fire once more to see my way back from the dark of what I thought was ordinary. Thank you, Kat.

Love is the cure, and allows us to be. Remember that through all of the harrowing journey you are about to take with us; that there are bright patches, and it does get better if you keep trying, and keep seeking awe in this world and beyond.

The Heroes' Journey and the 5 Stages of Grief

This poetry book has been formatted using an abridged scope of the Heroes' Journey, also known as the Monomyth, based on the structure popularised by Christopher Vogler, as well as the 5 Stages of Grief as developed by Elisabeth Kübler-Ross, a mental toolset first built to cope with the truth of a terminal illness.

With this ideal we also aim to teach a little about the many sections or thresholds of such a journey through each branch of this tale, and give you more context to the five stages of grief according to the Kübler-Ross model. Those stages are: Denial, Anger, Bargaining, Depression, and Acceptance; however, these steps do not need to be ventured in any particular order as is commonly believed, they come in waves and everyone experiences them differently.

The opposite of depression is expression, but the path to get there is never a straight line, never a direct route up the mountain. Control is birthed by that which has fear in their heart and mind, rather than love. Love is the root of trust, and community is the mission to hold sacred in opposition to the quest for personal glory in this Ordinary World.

Transformation begins at a place of AWE: Agency, Wonder, and Expression, and Time is our Only Obstacle to any kind of change - that is the core aspect of entropy, a natural law of reality. To change is to be one with the universe, and to grow is to let those parts of you that are no longer real, or, "a part of you", decay like broken branches of a tree to be alive, fully.

The Heroes' Journey details the Known World as the place that you begin, the Ordinary World where you define what is normal in a place that becomes anything but as a result of some harrowing event that takes away innocence and tears the poster from the wall.

The Unknown World is the place where the story evolves and becomes more perilous, when the Hero has taken the first steps past the Threshold, and into the place where the Heart of Darkness lies, where experience will be gained through Trials and Tribulations, and growth comes through that peril and decay of self-truth once deemed as absolute in the face of everything else.

Formatting of Fonts as Voices

* *Unknown Dark of the early ID = Powell Italic*
    Dreams and Desires that are not even known yet.

* Conflict of the Ego and ID = Dead History Roman
    Transference, Shame Spiraling, and Repression

* Known in the Light as Ego = National Park Regular
    The Self, Choice, Consciousness, and Individuality.

* future Light of the Superego = P22 Morris Troy & Golden
    Morals, Expectations, Pressures of the Social Contract, and the projected Ideal Self to fit into the metaphorical box.

* Conflict of the Ego and the Real World = Benguiat
    Aspects of (Undiagnosed) AuDHD Overwhelm, Delusions, Hallucinations, and DID Possession, among others.

* Conflict of the Ego and the Superego = Westsac
    Intrusive Thoughts and the DID Voice that comes from the Void within.

* My Shadow, according to Jung, where Ego and ID begin to merge and finally assimilate = Goldenbook Bold
    Balance from the Light cast from a healthier Superego and Dyadic connections.

Contents

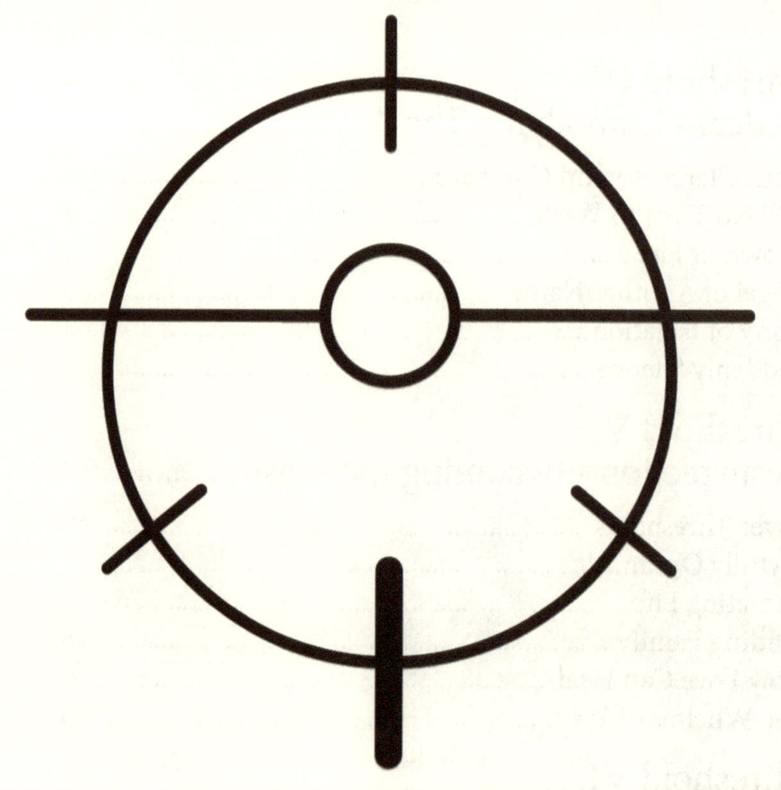

"Until you make the unconscious conscious, it will direct your life and you will call it fate."

~ *Karl Gustav Jung*

Threshold Null
Discovered in the Unknown World

How might one experience their journey if they didn't recall an Ordinary World to return to when Hell had subsided; when storms only pass for another storm to arrive?

Agency was lost in a world that cared little for how one exists outside of the consumerist ideal, or perhaps more approriately, the legacy of the family as a part of that system. Though there was love and moments of care; where does one go when they are emotionally abandoned for not following the dance exactly as it has been marked?

The first Threshold of the Heroes' Journey is where the tale begins; where the Ordinary World is understood and detailed. Where the stakes of the story have yet to be set, but bonds are understood. Those people, places, and truths keep them linked to themselves in later parts - unfolded.

This journey begins in the inverse, in the dark place. In that place of unknowing and discovery where I didn't understand and was separated from the ability to understand through unknown diagnoses of mental illness, AuDHD, and familial trauma that I would only resonate as truth in the 30th year of my life.

Thus, we begin by asking the most vital of questions as a primer poem and title of this book: *Which We is Me?*

Which We is Me?

Empathy through echoing masks. Voices, still...
   Trembling. Resting on high alert, and
   wrestling with the selves   that chase-
Past   the   Past catches up.   Who wins
                                                              this race at
                                                              the edge of
                                                              My Light?
   Who becomes me?   My Shadow?
   The abandoned Forest, at the edge of despair?   My Darkness?
   Fear clamboring like the mountainous shore -
   with tsunamis that break and drown my core.
Deluge upon the land, submerge my lair - please,
   oh please, don't take me back there.

      Who becomes me?
   The raging Dragon, who takes the fall?
   Burning all those that swell in my wake -
      who there dances in my squall?
   Legacy divined by righteous take -
      the King with wings of smog.

      Who becomes me?
   The hungry Werewolf, who runs in pacts?
   With fanged maw, and silent isolation,
      a natural predator with no hesitation.
   They who sees opportunity, survives -
   just one of the lies we sell most to thrive.

      Who becomes me?
   The darkened Eye, clouded in cosmic gas?
   That visage that can't stay inside -
   or **you** don't deserve to hide, or find trust,
      or to confide in anyone or anything.
My Dissonance berthed from the Void within.

Lose it all,
BE Lost,
LET ME IN.

Who becomes me,
if I'm not sure which We is me?
What mystery might We breed?

Who takes control,
if my me is adrift at sea?
What lives might We lead?

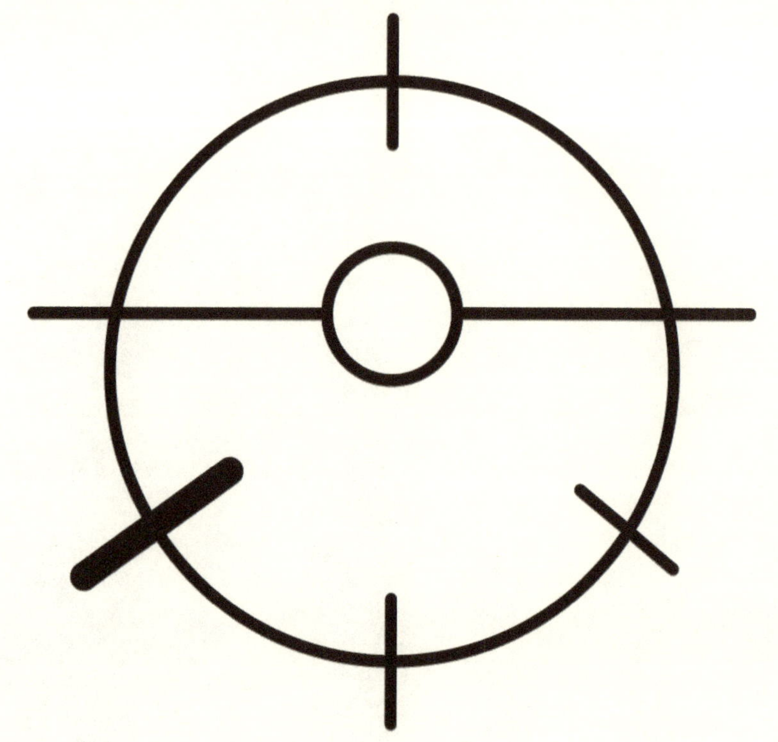

"Blind belief in authority is the greatest enemy of truth."

~Albert Einstein

Threshold I.
Separation ~ Hearing The Call

The poems from this chapter stem from truths hidden in youth, truths of the self that were reflected on through a process known as EMDR, or Eye Movement Desensitization and Reprocessing, a common therapy in Cognitive Behavioral Therapy or CBT, but also the shadow work of later years. Based on the ages of 6 to 12, these poems display the process of vacating that dark place where this inverted story begins.

Much like a phone, or radio, there is a wave of sound that one must hear, from within, to stand up and answer the call. It is a faint background noise unless a Champion can carry that voice forth into the darkness.

In other words, one might say that the "Signal was lost along the way", as heard in the song, *End of an Era* by Petri Alanko and Amelia Jones as featured in Alan Wake 2. In the context of the Heroes' Journey, this signal is also represented as the moment the "Call to Adventure" is heard, and it is often refuted when first heard by a Champion. By the time my child self came to discover it, I didn't have the perception of choice to make that decision. I had already begun self-adjusting.

It should not be a child's cause to be a Champion, and for that parentification, grief would accompany these occluded truths forward, beginning with denial. Denial in that the truth belongs to you, that it doesn't affect you, or that anything has even changed at all.

This stage is prolonged by technology like social media and social constructs that waylay our reflection of Death, and will remain as long as that contemplation is not committed to. The state of one's psychological mind and the fact that we will die one day is how to break this fragile and temporary structure of avoidance, but only with community to support you.

How Can Love Heal?

How does it feel,
to be loved? •   •   •

You mean, forced to heel?
To be broken like a beast,
a token of the feast - eat out my own heart from fear.
A symbol of the hand that feeds,
enclosed and entrenched with the impact of harsh deeds -
committed, chase now, the children in my charge.
Silent. Obedient. Don't you dare be large.
This is a part of my heritage.

Crack, goes the whip,
a metaphor studded in crystal,
but those gems don't define - which child he beats,
nor does the searing screams -
of overwhelm he bleats.
As the day falls to black,
as the drink cares not for who his fists find,
nor do the nightmares of shame - occupying his mind.

"He did the best he could."
Of course you would say that about him -
and for yourself, the same,
then go out and find
a new person   **THEN**
to blame.   he hurt him, and
FIRST
You hurt him and   he hurt me, so

I hurt them, and
so the cycle goes on.

Forever a device made to further Their plot,
whether for better weather, or legacies unfettered,
remember to love what you got - it could get wetter. Right?

Don't compare, don't despair, in fact, we'll have no empathy here -
                                    not in our divide.
Find another fellow to touch you inside.
With us you'll only find scars, bruises and where we had burned,
        wounds that are cheered with the right lessons learned,
            but we learned early that we weren't worthy.

Love, like respect is earned, we must provide value.
Have discipline and consequence, and only do things worthwhile.
        That means no art, nothing silver, only gold -
        only impact, and only those things that make us seem bold.
            If you're not shining then you don't exist;
            that was the next lesson on the list.

        Perfect or invisible, now a slave to stolen zeal.
        So, tell me again, how can *love* heal?

There Were Signs...

**IF YOU READ BETWEEN THE LINES,
YOU MIGHT COME TO FIND THAT:**

Far too attached to the idea of **T**ransparency.
Have never been **H**appier when I was fresh and clean.
Feeler of strong **E**motions, sensitive, and fragile, too.
Didn't fit into **R**eality, so I ran to fandom and fantasy.
Must be the leader, so I can make it **E**qual, justice be thy name.

Or else **W**ithdrawn, shy, quiet, and spacey.
Difficulty with **E**xpressing myself, at first, words were hazy.
My best friend was **R**esearching, so I could pass as "me".
My stories and **E**mpathy were different, too!

Opinionated, particular, or **S**tubborn, but always consistent.
Jokes that are **I**nappropriate or maybe even cringy.
Everytime I **G**abbed about my favorite plots, non-stop.
Constantly **N**ervous, or else I end up lazy.
Even when I was **S**upported, I still couldn't listen.

.
.
.

Entitled to Question

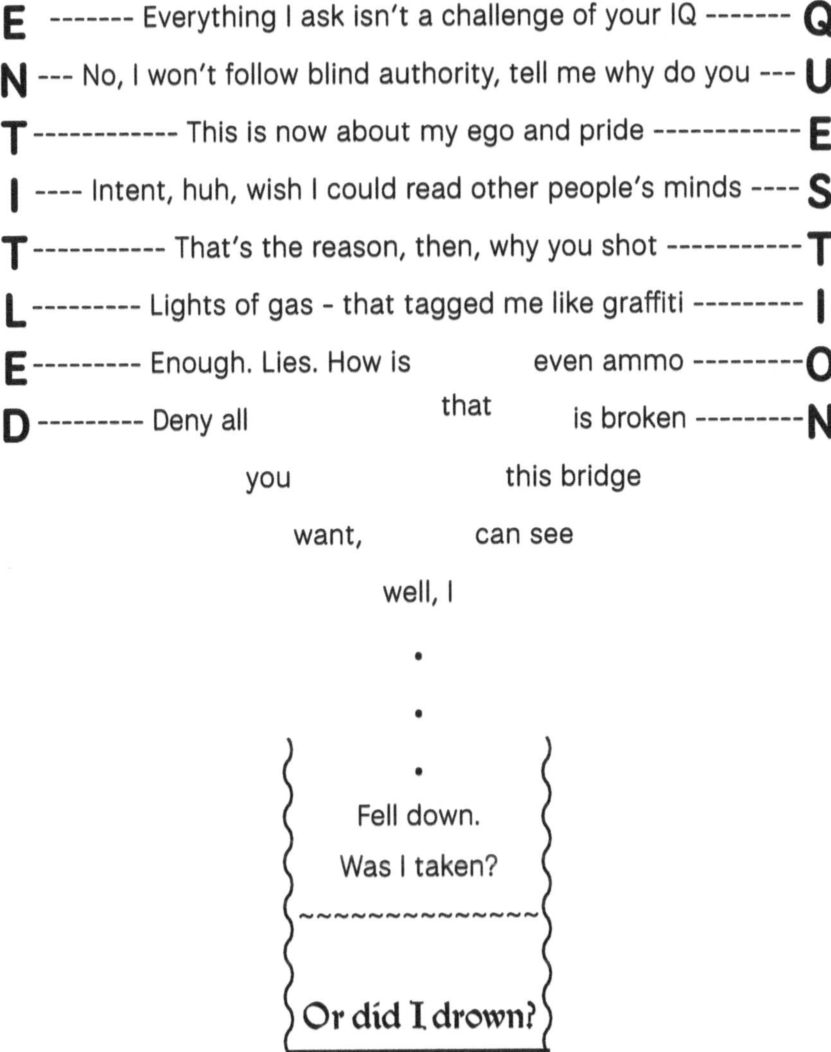

Breaking Beauty Because...

Autumn in recess -
    words turn into regrets | Snap!
       Where did the time flow?

Here I go...

Action lost in haze -
    harbor dark water and find -
       blackout by new rage.

Beauty Broke,

Bonds are severed now,
    cut by a tether I can't -
       quench the flame inside.

Because Why?

Halls of Gods and Heroes

Shot in the Dark, Legacy to share,
   then save me 'fore I discover the Mare!
The Ode of Legacy it stings, as the cries of those below you,
   whose screams you hear, it sings,
      and now haunts those tides of umber,
         which used to fondly be called dreams.

Four pillars atop, a foundation that rots Royalty,
                      a disguise for all to see,
   as a visage of Heroes, easy to claim,
     as the idealized beasts; outside - with which to tame.
   Ringing with a Bell that is made of
   what seems like light and sound,
     but sours with a sickly round,
           a dark concerto, a blinding conservatory -
   this is the Hall where Legacy is found.

All else matters little in this Hall of Gods and Heroes,
   They are the House and They win the game,
     and They who wins writes the Story.
   The Story told as if the Word of God,
     sits alongside in judgement and fury.

And what a Story, They matched it with a plinth!
   Stone that once held my fathers' name -
   face, and tag, scratched out long before I was hatched,
     as just a baby in rags among Dragons -
     but that's not the song they sing,
       only the toll of the Bell gone mad,
         the loud-ticking tocks, and chiming hells
         that stem from this Hall.
       Time and Thought is the villain of all Legacy -
     Lost the plot, let's get back to the Story...
   Back to the plinth, of my Father the day,

They decided he, too, was no longer worthy.
Twisted and shaken, sensitive, mistaken,
   like father like son, I suppose.
So there was I, lonely and weak, at an ivory tower in the Sun,
   I was broken and meek, but told that I didn't have to be,
   by Dragons with horns and devilish scales -
   how the tale came to look to me.   I tried too...

Become all of the things They said he could no longer seek -
and he believed Them.

                                    Why Would I Feel Any Different?
How could you not?   Who doesn't want to be special?

How could you not want to be singing with the bells
and finding your face in this happy-adorned place,
   with pictures and memories plastered all over the wall,
      proof of something more pleasant,
         something glittering and adoring -
         something I couldn't earn as a peasant.
   They made that apparent, but who's to blame?

                              Not They.

Nothing is pleasant about being an orphan,
   especially when no one knows it, not even
                              yourself.

Maybe something was once there,
      but outlining the box and telling me to fit in or fail -
      made it easy to keep denying.
Time to start the next bonfire,
         in case I do fail -
         to carve enough of myself away to be
         small enough for Them to handle
                              me.

   The offer still stands, to be the one They demand,
      to shield this blade of unwieldy commands,
         black-white-shaped-steel;
            though the tock and the bell still stalk,
               so now let's listen to the Matriarch...

Give thy life to thee and cull!
    Cut thine self from thine self,
        to save thine self from thou father's Penny Dreadful!

I mean... this squalor and filth, see our columns and beds?
Don't you want to be part of what I built, instead?
    Beauty and bright, knowledge and that's right,
        we do have trust, funded to make it here one day,
            but not until you earn it – trust as well as the money.
        Don't you want to see what I see – all this...
        potential for something different?

Make a stake of Legacy and try to take the rung of this ladder that
will be hung just out of your scope and reach,
    a rite of passage,
        along with your silver-green spoon that will give way to
        jealousy from siblings.

We are all you have,
    you can't pick your family,
        so stick to the creed and welcome now,
            to this life of power (fear) and greed (envy).

Fountains of wealth and long lasting health,
the last two pillars of Legacies remain –
You must abandon your Self, as acceptance proves guilt,
    and the last one comes as no surprise –
    its pride and ego, set to be slain, no longer felt,
        to make way inside, the hollowed out
        envy-green sanctuary I used to hide.

                            those last real parts of me
    Not the God or Hero, They made me out to be.

Island of Trees

climbs -

The rocky hillside   beckoning, pleading to feed -
  send another to the shelter of the vane,
    the victim is the seed.

  Though the Forest did stem, a sanctuary from him,
    what was the crop that grew up past the brim,
      if not that sullied length of rope?
    The vines embraced, and hung this boy,
      strung him up by his own false hope,
      right into that sloped spiral.

Those vines and thorns that dug and scorned,
  drank up all his misery - even those dreams marked as viral.
Their thirst then teemed, befitting it seemed,
  as trees, and leaves, and lush vallies,
    hunger for a home in cities, too.
They made a shelter of his faith -
  and made him feel like new.
    As a mighty tree, soulful, silent and stout -
    another wood of the weald, ever stoic in doubt.

Time is our only obstacle,
    a construct we've all shared.
        Written by Death, who waits for no one,
            so live life as one. Don't be scared.
                Break the cycle, it's not a loop, reinvent the wheel;
                    find your Self, at long last, and
                        then see how you feel.

Afraid. The light is fright, alright,
    now, with verdant devoured,
        the mountains are scoured -
        no longer avoiding my lair.
        The Forest unlocked a haven, a hold,
            a gate to unfold, and divine myself into -
            but never a witness to bear.
            He became the tree that fell in that Forest,
                one which was never heard,
                one which stemmed an ocean of others;
                flourished by grace not yet conferred.
                The seed from his heart, unseen,
                    twas ripped apart, root and bark,
                    and scattered like ashes to the green.

Deny the truth, deny the self, even deny the pain -
    the first step laid, was the first step made
        for me to become insane.

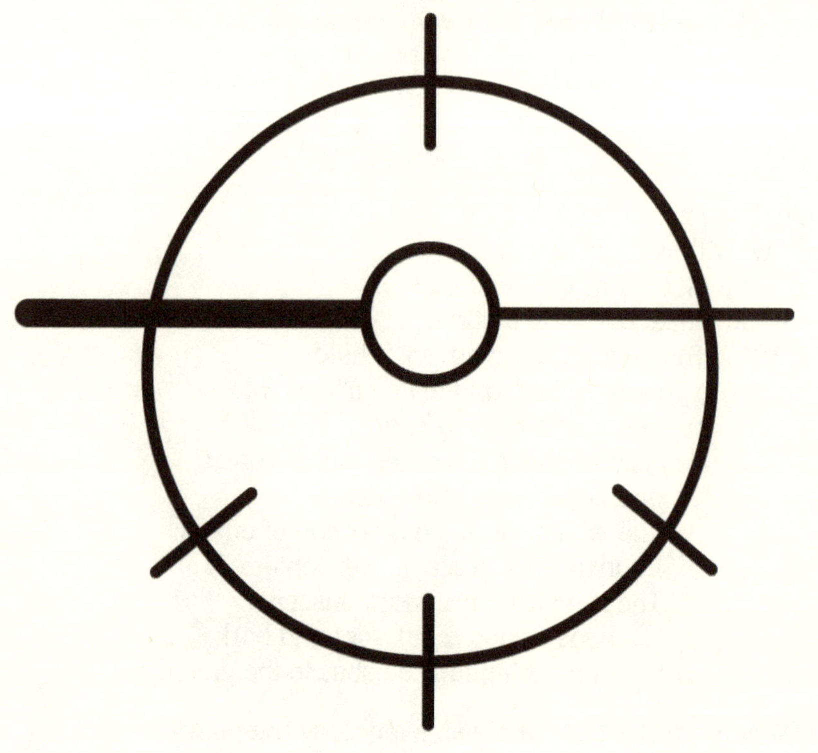

"Come not between the dragon and his wrath!"

~*Shakespeare's King Lear, Act 1 Scene 1*

Threshold II.
Aid - Taking The Fall

As we journey onward, we discover the next stage of the story where mentors are instead sparse and hidden away. The quest begins without that fated signal heard from above to continue with patience and grace. This is the place these poems come from, continuing from early youth to the time the state came to split me and my brothers from our father, and away me to my mother.

In the Heroes' Journey, the place where the journey enters the darkness and the unknown is referred to as the "Threshold", and as one "Crosses this First Threshold", they are meant to be ready to take on the challenges that lie before them - only in this case, the threshold comes without aid, as we enter that Ordinary World.

Without that mentorship and acceptance of "The Call" one becomes composed of not only that darkness but also anger as they believe and are shown time and time again that they are unable to change the truth of their quest and situation. Anger is also the next stage in grief, and stems that same root of frustration incarnate.

Rage at the unfairness of it all, anger at the compounded blame of the self for being stuck in the loop of knowing the truth but being unable to change it, and fury in the wondering of how such a tragedy could even occur. Awareness is only part of the equation, action is the other half.

This stage of grief can only begin to change when one gains wisdom through reflection and by breaking the cycle. It is one of the most difficult tasks in life, for when you scream into the Void of this loop long enough, it begins to feedback in kind until all spirals out of control.

Comparison's Bedfellow

Who goes there, apple of my eye, burnt orange
    and spotted, and filled with such lies!?
But painted oh so sweetly, are all those visions and whys,
    who am I? The question escapes my lungs,
        who am I? A question asked of my young, Self. So I -
          am my own imposter conjured by the tongues 'cause -
        of the Matriarch who lives on high,
          separate from those among us.

The pretender within is born from my kin.
Preaching that to be Me, is a grievous sin,
    so I let that most dark ambition in,
    it filled me up, and cracked my cup,
        it gave a new Voice and settled therein -
          something that was meant to be
          better than the me I could ever see.
My own thief of joy is this reflection contained,
a bedfellow of that mission it claims - a contrast.
Of me to me and thee and We and
all ye Gods that I have had to give up on.
    We writers make our own apogee,
    after all, in name and in game,
        the MVP of this rhythm detained -
        he and I are one in the same,
          but We just don't know that yet.

Slay the Ego Super or else my ID.

Being in this future is what keeps me blinded,
    and histories so ancient they shan't be recorded,
    or stories so far forward I won't be reminded,
    of who I was before being ordered,
        to be the Hero of them all - or shunned.

•

•

•

I guess I'm to be the Chosen One.

Oh, what fun, to sit there and compare my stares in the mirror -
to a who I don't want to be, that looks like my father,
    but that wasn't a bother, until They sealed my fate.
    They simply made an example of
        who he was and who I am,
            not unlike a venn diagram,
                an equation of unequal, a sequence of some evil -
                telling me to be the leader of each and every sequel.
                Even those that aren't mine, but why? Easy...

Because no one can do what I do -
the golden boy, the son of ploys,
    the twisted mister, who is cruel
    and destroys   -   Truths that aren't Ours!
        anything that doesn't matter to the Legacy,
            even the book says you have to be,
                under me... less than, don't you see,
                    they told me to slay, so I must obey.
                For this is how I be Their Hero someday,
                    by doing what this other me would do.
                from laying a trap, and taking a lap,
                    when I have finished my conquering of You.

Awaken now as my own dark dream -

I think we'll make an eXcellent team.

No Time to Waste

How long it's been since I first heard the tock,
the resonant sound of the ticking clock-
the scale and measure of Gods and Heroes,
the multiplier which resets all back to zero?

Whoosh!

A rush of wind, the air was cinder, brimstone-hot,
the heat wave inside would collide with tinder...
This was our best kept secret that lied - in wait, with that whisper,
that crisper vision being a part of that blessing -
in disguise, it lessens nothing, yet;
only amplifies the Else I already saw in my,
glimmer of the distant, darkened,
misted third Eye.

atop my chest,
Always playing with the pressure mounted, a perspective that's
not quite... grounded -
born from cursed futures
atop my crest.

The moment she went and made the call - I was chosen,
and would take the fall - **a Hero who just didn't know it.**
So, remember the Hall and the bell that was cast, well
that shit evolved, and now it resolved,
to fell me for **sins I must bear.**
Don't let me idle, as I've run miles and miles,
and have **no idols** to spare.
They showed me, that to unfurl, We'd play "Me Against the World",
a part and role I've had to learn well -
Enough, alone. Not scared, right? Just...

Hyperaware
Of how -
Pressure Makes
Diamonds **Perfect.**
Flawless so it is -
the fate -

I seek from borrowed ambition that burns,
what darkness yet yearns to fallow -
from those once-and-jaded ferns.
Those trees you recall, from the days of old -
        so aside from the Hall,
they can't offer us sparks now, I'm told.
So the well that once held rain could no longer contain -
        nor isolate -
        only condemn and hate, as a pool of my own boiling blood.
A terrible torrent, a monsoonal flood,
        simmering and soldering the scraps, fractured to become -
        something sharp and something stronger...
                She said I couldn't be me any longer...
                                Only Perfect.

And, I really am sorry for the big reveal - this time -
        but the light was quite clear, foresight's just another of
        those blessings from my patron,
                I fear -

Ican'twaitfortheweightoftheworldtogetoffmybeing -
I told you I can see the future, but I'm only human.

Only Human   ONLY HUMAN

A Cog with no Kami

Knowledge is Power, unchecked it devours,
not a slave to Wisdom forsworn.

Thus, the Wall was constructed,
the view it obstructed is only imagined, not born.

Great! |

The Wall towers, a tempered gate, too, it dours,
    an empty which drug o'er my core,
Still then stands, as a bridge-once, it demands might -
    to enter or climb o'er the great door.

But wait -
    a daunting gauntlet was thrown beyond the gate with no flight;
        because of a Cog with no Kami.
    Not oiled or reared from once-molten steel,
    so theres no defect of the foundry -
        this ore failed to mesh with any sprockets or gears -
        as a vessel with no roots or peers around it.

The Wall | All it can defend, all it tries to mend,
    like memories from another land - or, another self,
        under chevroned hoods, trying to
        keep it all in hand - or hidden.
No. Not that one. Buried.
Out of sight. Keep it buried - in that box;
under that fifth wall, or was it the sixth?

I forget which one sunders heaven -
Or which one makes home feel like prison -
And kept us bored to steal our levin -
The box is one we formed ourselves in.

From those dreams, and hopes, and things unseen,
    that sit on the shelf safely, marked with "familiarity".
The Wall keeps us from that edge, with clarity -
perspective of "out of sight" and "out of mind".
    Then... that's how we fell unkind, I see.

The gate remains, I suppose,
    and should never impose the Engineer inside,
        who once held a heart made of true gold;
        while the silver gauntlet,
        too passed, still lies in the grass,
            a hand with no other to hold.

    So, the cog in the wall became dark and drawled,
            but once sat upon - as a spirited ring.
    Since this bond of the past, the metal aged fast,
                alas, a once-splendid thing.

        Twas now twisted and marred
        with gruesome black scars,
            a monument to that hopeful sin.
        Ruin was next, as the hand it was set for,
            made him yearn too deep for his yin.
        Thus he became, this broken and lame,
            Engineer of love, no more.

Awake Atop the Mare

A lack of sleep, a lack of dreams, nothing is as what it seems.
The day is night, the light slips to grey - the dreams
come back, please just stay away.
        Ever lurking, ever working, a dream with no rest -
        I mean, restless, like the Mare - the one who I saw...
            Oh, you don't see it there?

                                            Am I Dreaming?

        Nevermind, but then how the fuck did we get here?
How the hell... did it ring my bell, or have I always been unsung?

What I remember first was dying of thirst,
where we would then just appear?
So, I gave it my crest, and from the Void
it rest, a curse 'pon my soul with one glare.
Then, I just was, and on the Mare 'cause,
I guess that we had to use fear?
Atop of this umber, I had no number -
equal, as a lonely pair.

                        Is this a Vision?
                        Who's talking?

That was all I can recall, before the abyss and the fall,
        where I lost the reins, then lost the light,
        and in that span I met my fright -
        a billion of me compounded - into one -
chest, with only a fragile, little beating thing. A hollow, tiny,
corrupted ark, a container without a soul or spark - stolen or
was it ever there? The terror could not stay in that box forever, no
vessel to hide or hold, and all bad things must come to an end, or
so the story's told.
That means **you**, too, **you know.**

                                    What is stalking us?
        It's too late to play pretend,
            like the link isn't lost once again.
        Trace my steps backwards, for a time -   after time;
                        where I wasn't asleep,
                        where there was no maze,
                        when we weren't afraid of the deep,
                        or what was birthed within that haze.

I know what sings in those dark tones, cacophonies of crispened whispers, and even subtle drones; because their own became my tone and pen... Where was I again?

Oh, yeah, if I told you about my flying horse, you'd know I'm not sane, so yeah, it's just a story. A metaphor, you know, a parable.
    I don't really think there is a creature looming at the door.
    The threshold, the one that you say, I have to have the
    courage to walk through someday. Even though there are
    true beasts, monsters like They, standing here in the light of
    day. Wolves in sheep's attire, no, that's not right, it's clothing!

Keep Trying, Keep Going!

Fuck you, it's not fair! Yes, tell them how **you** feel,
        unlock those gates of hate that broil and rumble,
      show this life what it's like when They take a tumble.

How come I have to have the courage to do what you won't do? Watch me break the Sun, instead, like you taught me how to - the truth hurts, so let's just cower and simmer like the coals of ire that tower like rooks of fire in the head - of my Nightmare - but the hue burns with orange not red?

Where are the brakes on this thing?

Wait, I don't know if my psyche can take another one, so let's keep going, and going, and going until we reach the end. Of what? I think I'm there already.
I give up -
        Just stay steady, balanced, and stand -

There **you** are **you** pesky star - **you** don't belong here as what **you** are. Can't have **you** giving him more of that unruly rope, no, no, no more of that false hope - he tried, and he tried, but now it's high time for low tide. No more waves, no more swells, not one ounce of happiness until - until I have control and he lets me win, he's nothing more than my hollowing, dark shell.

Speak again and I'll see **you** with me, here, in this Hell!

Frozen–

Once-carved of naught but rock and teal-Ice,
how can I make you see -
This system was made to be precise.

How else can I be concise...
I know I'm not the only extrasensory!
Who's carved of rock'n teal-Ice

Not one made to roll the dice -
to things ambiguous or temporary.
This system was made to be precise.

How to tell what to sacrifice?
Hyperfocus is the lock and key -
To carve the rock'n teal-Ice.

Look at how I did it thrice!
Routines, and patterns are compulsory.
This system was made to be precise.

The crushing claw of social vice -
My perpetual catastrophe.
Once-carved of naught but rock'n teal-Ice.
This system was made to be precise.

-Fire

Take this stake of ash-red Flame,
    from two sides that never agree -
Loose track of my timeframe.

I find interest to the point of maim -
Let's not forget bouts of impulsivity!
Take this stake of ash-red Flame.

 It's much more fun inside a game -
where can I go fly free?
Losing track of my timeframe.

What was I doing before I became?
Frozen here burning for all eternity -
Take this stake of ash-red Flame.

Bright, but the light's never the same.
Where did all those thoughts flee?
Lost track of my timeframe.

Here now it falls, the spiral of shame,
    so I call out one final plea.
Take this stake of ash-red Flame.
Bereft of my timeframe.

Left and Right pages can either be read
on their own OR reading lines from the
pages on both sides together as one line.

To Dance With Dragons

What desert do I wake in, with a trace of stolen greed?
What path less-travelled did I walk, that made me lose my seed?
I trod and trot until I stalk, a ghost of fumes, unseen.
    As this barren gorge had only forged things brown,
        and not those found in green.

Forget about the other side, I still hold that envy-vile,
    of better than what I was before -
    but a branch of that broken tree-isle.
        Reach the tor, mount of fury and languor -
        beset by smog most foul,
            a brightness shielding haze.
        We shan't pass Their test of whisper and prowl,
            as less-light wielding rays.

Flush with that ride of umber, slumbering like my Mare,
    even though I'm unaware - of just how -
        the Sun does rest, lurch and lumber,
            carved from circle to square.
How does one go from one to the other, or another, you wonder?
    Well, the mask is cut from cloth once wrought,
        and dead wood left asunder.
    Then it carves a shape, hewed and hemmed -
    stained for all to see,
        made of blood and tooth and nail it mends those scars of We.

The grooves of the mask became much like the scratch -
        of a song and rhythm that once had turned tail.
Record belief echoing - Hero, a single with no pair to match -
    setup to be struck, sparked, then erupt,
        and fall with no flame to catch.

Swept up in that tide, of riches and ides,
    to become the very thing that we spurned;
        though lessons were made as those that They yearned -
            for, I learned how to take on the eternal dance,
                from the masters, the Dragons - my lords.

Time is our only obstacle,
        a construct we've all shared.
            Written by Death, who waits for no one,
                so live life as one. Don't be scared.
                    Break the cycle, it's not a loop, reinvent the wheel;
                    find your Self, at long last, and
                    then see how you feel.

Like a broken viol, or a harp strung so tight that it snaps from the
pressure it struggles to fight - like a broken melody or song you hum
along to, or something that screeches and stutters in two or three or
four or more. It starts on cycles that cry "repeat" - a feedback that utters
and loops around on itself, itself, yourself, again, and again, once again

> Remember that **you still don't have any friends.**

There it was, on the other bend, the Volcano with abyssal depths and
rivers that flow deep and never do quite end. There it awaits to strike the
right chord and shutters the fjords, then cause the earth to quake from
silent might and peaks that rise up steep.

Follow the buzzards that reveal our despair - the only rule is survival
out here... The only rule is survival out here. In the real world - that's
normal. This wasteland is a path in life's journey, twas said, one They
went through so... tis only fair I tread, those same pits, but then... spite
had nothing to do with it!

> Too late, **you** gave them too much credit -

I realize, so the rage consumes, and spreads - flowing within to fuel
black-red-jet-flamed-dread that dulls thine edge and flattens thine
aspect. That ought to teach me a little respect;

Mirroring dark glares of shame - is that my own reflection?
That Void holds those parts They rejected -
like a defection of our Self perfected.

Fear so sweet it's like a confectioners' delight - of frenzied fright and
hate and fate intertwined; like the dust of rust from iron sands and
forlorn lands which only abate this psychic storm with a tributary dance
of blood performed. It rains evermore as the scars streak across my
soles from atop forbidden, muddied, scarlet lye belonging to those
mighty serpents up on high - the soap of the histories and heroes that
they scrubbed to come out clean, squeaky and sightly.
The machine for white-washing run with the Moon, nightly.

The next step laid could only be made with wisdom from crimson
pearls. Anger of a miraged King, horned; wings of red-black.

> Who gives shelter to the scorned?

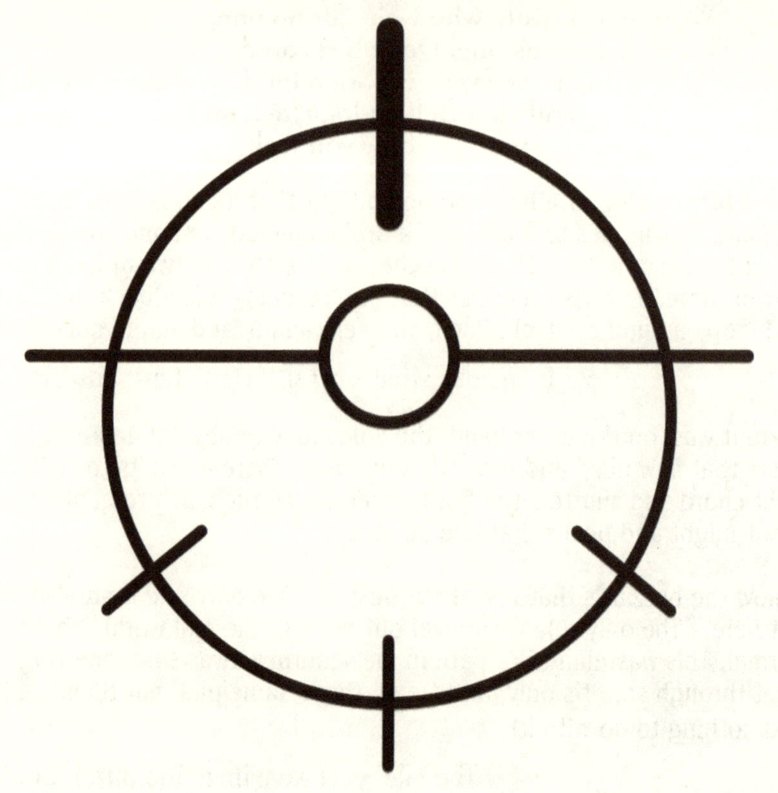

"The first rule of business is: Do other men for they would do you."

~ *Charles Dickens*

Threshold III.
Initiation - Surviving The Trials

Venturing onwards again, the quest enters the next fateful branch. With no time to prepare or advance in safety; these poems detail cycles discovered in High School and Young Adulthood. Learning to distrust all; especially those that claim to care for and love me. I grew up in paranoia, plagued with a blinding loneliness under the Sun.

That loneliness was ironically not on its own as long term ailments suffered through Chronic Kidney Disease (CKD) and End-Stage Renal Disease (ESRD) were joined by the start of the steepest decline into Dissociative Identity Disorder (DID). This became the next truth. In sickness and relative abandonment, I succumbed to Death; even being claimed for a brief moment in time before all of these truths were discovered.

The context of the Heroes' Journey is marked at this point as the space where "Tests, Allies, and Enemies" are found, favored, and survived, and is the final step before "Approaching the Innermost Cave" - the darkest part of that dark place where light has never dared to touch.

For now; though, "the Hero" must bargain for a life spent, as well as a life owed. Bargaining is the next stage of grief, too, and begets desperations that are impossible to quantify when you've met an end that was once craved, but savored no longer. In this dealing with Death, one must find a new belief in themselves. Then, they may see beyond the Void they relinquish themselves to.

Glimmers of Affection

How does it feel?
To be wolfed down, as if a meal?

Lust and love unwind me, as I become
the bridge for want and consume -
my spirit given freely, until I too was numb
as light without boundaries, became my foundry and tomb.

These glimmers of lust had many a host
seeking to fill my Void from somewhere.
Luckily, love would not be a ghost,
in showing I'm not past repair.

Expectation now set, a zero and let -
me keep my damned tongue in check,
as it speaks smut and my other secret.
That I'm little more but a desperate wreck.

More than a kiss, found in each seal.
Tell me again, how can love heal?

Alone at Long Lost

Molded among the dark-blue-grey smog-smoke-mist—How can one hope to trust the process?—Low, so start now,—a moment of silence, that is reminisced. — No feeling of love, alone to profess.—Climbing the hill, we're stuck at the twist.—you've faded from memory, thanks to the mist.—A feeling of warmth, once reminisced.—that is unless — this tale with a twist! — If one should tread lightly, then, they could enlist,—a moment of warmth, once reminisced.—Why does one even try to persist?—As below so above, one could not assess,—blinded by the smog and thick, living mist. —The call sings, it hums, it's hard to resist—this was never a safe place of egress —so how do you suppose one would likely progress?—Nearly a dearly departed now—kiss goodbye, see one final twist. — The paths all gone, it hides, as Death seeks a new tryst,—With memories jaded, oozing the grey mist—Oh, hedonist fall fast, become the last twist! — Spent at the end of a match made that cost, — my everything's gone here,

Alone at Long Lost... — Find us there, give in and exhaust. — We found them to establish the link. Looping forever from the opposite sync. Who we are now is anyone's guess... Pull us away, taken and drowned on the brink. — To create my "Me" from that token link. Then deny and repress "The Creator", but only in red ink. — Then spiral down this quagmired sync; which is where these waves do oppress. Try not to fall into that dark drink. — There it is, a bond made, a link! — He thinks sleep is now for the weak, made for dreams to confess. — Then let's wait a moment, his ego will shrink. — The signal is lost, reality's still in sync. Prepare ourselves, in fact, we're eager to bless - then bind You inside that neurotic clink. — Time to mend this broken link, for he must be ready now, primed to possess. Send the dark smog now, make the last sync?

Fade to Blue

Where dost thou march and wade to?
Through the smog that's dark-blue, and greyed who –
mixed with mist and smoke of shade,
        then cropped atop this arced crusade;
            where have thou gone, thine debts are still not paid!

The fog climbs inside so thine attunes to blindness.
It swelled within, sealed by thine skin,
crossing mires with the madness –
        a cascade that strayed, then laid therein,
            this rising tide up to thy chin –
                may fluid of the whelm fill thy lungs.
Death lay claim no accolades, but still will claim a soul that clung;
        just thou wait and see – for whom the bell rings and tolls.
In truth we've only just entered the cave, the one with steam
from orange coals.
Now is thine chance, thou can't afford the lance,
        or shield that's adorned in blue-like trance.
A grown child alone in the maze.

Take mine life now, please, make the trade!
To settle the matter of mind over Ye,
        the one incepted inside that old tree.
Too young to plant a truth like that –
Too late to build up a team, a brigade,
Thou Lost them in thine: Glory, Wrath, and Memory preyed.
So Death will take the trade, one for many, in objectivity.

Shattered relief comes alongside a broken belief, a hero and truth in one,
        but only by a palisade, made to hew the oldfound facts undone.
In this tower shield-tall was a staff of power,
        twisted with two snakes inlaid,
            a newfound vow to thrive, not just survive;
                then it seemeed the lance of medicine slayed it after all!
        Though in a moment just too late...
The lance and shield broke the blade with little force made,
        but not until a moment after that masquerade of Death;
makes this past me draw their last breath... then Fade to Blue....
        to see nothing on the other side...
        just a black-orange-purple-toned hue,
        the abstract meshing of my I's.

Then suddenly a wolf and bright glade!

Through the woods now...
	with white light bathed from above, is that enough,
		may my debt be paid? Is that why you've shown me this place?
			Is it alright to stand in this circle now, and not a box?

Alone in bed now - a break is not evaded,
							I'm scared.
I know I'm not here because I dared to pray past the pervading...
	never saw a point in it, but one could say to beg's much the same....
	This grove appears to be without that power, greed, or shame?

Look, the twin snake, they made it, too!
And the wolf, how it sings such a serenade,
	a chorus for a pack of more than just You, but that is for another day,
		one in the far-flung future-true.

				I never noticed how much I love it's howl.
First we must find who had to persuade Death
for a life to end to save mine;
	a love that can't be defined.
							The curse began to break thus,
	the serpents had found a worth in us - and gave a new life to find.
				A new future... but first these tubes and bags and scars.
	Proof I'm not Perfect, but wow, would you look at those stars...

A Damp, Whetstone

For almost a quarter of that year,
    the glade returned me to a pack,
        one that had once scattered to the leaves for fear -
        of the sharp tongue formed in desert flamed-attack;
        fellows who wear the same pelts of shame-branded,
            but can't understand the battle I just went through.
    And neither really knows what's in store,
        but I made it back from the Southern shore - somehow...

Silver-blue stars still chase dreams along the Moon,
    but the tune soon changes from tube-ridden places,
        cycling blood from my deepest core underground.
Dialyze my catalyst to shift this form,
    react like a chemical to mold the cyst within -
    I'll take the poison to stop myself, and hold in limbo my sin.
The brain fog keeps those lights of gas at bay;
    of course, it can't stop storms all day.
There They crawl! Like scratches and scrawls -
rearranging the halls that abscond my mind -
    and smiting the Sun we just bade.
Losing the sight, blind from all other sides, this would let the Evil Eye in, so...
    Lo, a meteor from through the gloomy clouds,
        the metal for a new sword or blade is found!
    Something I didn't know we needed,
        but don't you feel it thrum and flow -
        this is not like the other ore, or the edge it gave!
Thus the new forge is made away from this circle of love and pure grace,
    but only as is custom.
Then a cabin is formed along the river, complete with a mill of whelm,
    a clearing is culled aside a grassy gnoll,
                the Engineer stands at the helm.

Above those columns of lofty shade,
    pulses a glimmer of dark orange awake;
        like a whetstone where the heart of gold once laid -
    a fission where Super and Ego both stake.
This whetstone damp would sharpen blades, and dry would give way to fire;
    which then serves to temper the sword - built to be broad, not a bastard.
Obsession bartered to settle the score,
to the stain the pen might have contained...
    an acknowledgement, to those stories of light not quite mastered, or laid.
            Howling as a lone wolf of the glade.

Let Me (W)in!

Are you up yet? Good, then let's get started.
   Another fine day as the living departed.

Already, I just opened my eyes,
   and I'm unsteady, unstable,
      a product ready to give up my seat at the table,
         so here goes the fable of my imaginary friend(s) imprisoned -
      they're pretend, but quite capable on occasion.

A million, million Voices. Or... are they echoes? Then,
there's still eons of whispers left to go.   Save for One.
Fostering phantasy, with varied notes and flow;
   those which scarcity made it fair to be a -
   soldier of these crucibles of parity,   Can You hear me?
     or, was it just another tragedy,
to go deaf from silent decibels?

I guess we'll never know...   I am still here, don't go!

   ] -
Discover that-shifting part-
   the werewolf skin adorning me-a symbol of my fealty.
             Yield now
             And forever hold
your contempt for- your peace for- your breath for-   loyalty to the Dark I?
Yes, that sounds right, it is Eye.
Who sees what They see, your selfish need to break free from this
kingdom which you could hold the key to if only you would just do as
They say, but you don't and you won't, not anymore, not with me here,
not today. Stay atop that steed of impulse and split apart the You tree inside
you with your stomach all in knots, and drive a stake into your own
hearthwood core, you brambled beast, but only if you get unruly... Eye'll
let you know alright, justly and truly. Trust me, I'm your only friend.

       Now, go ahead, let me in.
You're not real. I just don't know that yet.
       If I'm not real, then neither are you.
Wait, where is that soulful melody singing from?
   It sounds like it's missing something.
     That would be someone, it's true. You want this to be
   You, and Me, and We in our Black Hole for all of Eternity.

Ah -
So, that's where the whispers climb to, humming tunes so sweet,
    so full of color, all but one, I think, but oh then hear -
        it's meter and rhythm, and it all plays in time,
        a symphony of perfection - save for that one little... thing missing...
            Something's Missing... what is missing?

                              lyrics and rhyme

I can't stop humming along because it's right on the edge,
    the edge of Occam's razor,
        it's so simple, so brilliant -
        now I'm focused, no longer the pupil!
    Why didn't I see it before!? But...
        then why is it still not sounding right...
            is it the form, or did the Engineer do something grand-like -
            shape it askew? I don't... understand.

That's it, that's true! That other version of **you** took it from **you**, and
changed the words into this twisted mix, it wasn't Eye, the one who is
always here by **your** side, taking care of **you**, in every way that makes
you seen - I'm not alone in here, **you** know what I mean.

              Cough

The air is getting thin, so I'll just keep popping neurons until you let me in;
until you just give up, or you let me win.

Tonight's not the night, we've been at this all day,
    maybe tomorrow, maybe there is no way -
    to finish this song that no one else plays or hears.
        A felonious droning that conjures Their dark fears,
            and patches the scars with visages and jars -
            to bottle up all the bad things - it sings and bars -
            the way for me to reach the next day.
Tomorrow you'll see, I'll conquer this tune.
    Don't believe that, give it up you stark, raving loon,
        What was that?   You hear it too?

not without lyrics you can't, not anytime soon.

Pacts of Werewolves

Beware the Black Shifter of Dread!
A beast not born and not bred,
aspect of the Full Moon -
Might not be tonight, but soon...
you'll find it on your stead!

How sick it is to reside
 in a country drowning in crowds as it stands -
 on the back of those who are in silence,
  and those who are dead and free of commands:
   The creedo of those who employ violence, and make demands;
   as They claim to know all that is right and all that is true.
  They say forget your truth, as They make you commit Their
   atrocities, too.
  That's how we survive, in a system of work or die,
   where survival becomes fitness, a ritual to witness,
    the climbing of that invisible ladder. Subtext is power.
   In or out, time to be the best performer.
   "Act natural", or "fake it 'til you make it", or...

Become one with the pact, this Den of Werewolves,
and try this shifting skin on -
 it fits like a glove because it's commonplace,
  this complacency, and indifference to humanity.
 Surrounded by metal and glass,
  foundations that smash the earth, cleaved under their heel,
   stalagmites that rise as shaped-sharped-bits of towered steal.
   Man-made mountains to look down at the world on.
 We are just animals who think that we've won -
  this race of evolution -
  but class, and racial divides make it simple -
  to separate ourselves from this voice we find dying deep inside.
The Death throes of hope I have not...

What, given up? That is a lie, you give up all the time, the time in the world, filtering through your mind, that is why I am; because you can't see, you can't see what They see, so give up and let me be, then I'll be free to reign terror on those who aren't you! I know that's what you want, to give up for good, I'm right here inside with you, you fool. Not a critic, but something more real, a Voice with only a body to steal. Yours, and you will Let me Win in the end, a side of your own, alone with no friends. It's not too late, let's make those amends...

Time is our only obstacle,
      a construct we've all shared.
           Written by Death, who waits for no one,
                so live life as one. Don't be scared.
                    Break the cycle, it's not a loop, reinvent the wheel;
                        find your Self, at long last, and then see how you feel.

I feel – empty now, a vessel of the dark cloud incarnate, my eyes go from
white to black with the world as I go on attack – as the mongrel now.
The one that's been chained in the yard for its whole life, unleashed.
Let flesh render the image of myself on the other side of this shape-
shifting blessing that I have taken on. Changing with each room I creep
through, sweeping up myself like how a broom cleans up a mess, and I
am never clean.

Never have been clean, They say, so tell me then, what's really changed?
Take the next step, a wolf still lost with no pack, a fact,
    so watch as I spiral to my natural state of deranged,
        and give up as I sign the pact...
        Fuck, even the survivalist gives up some day.

Thank Eye, We're so tired of all your wordplay.

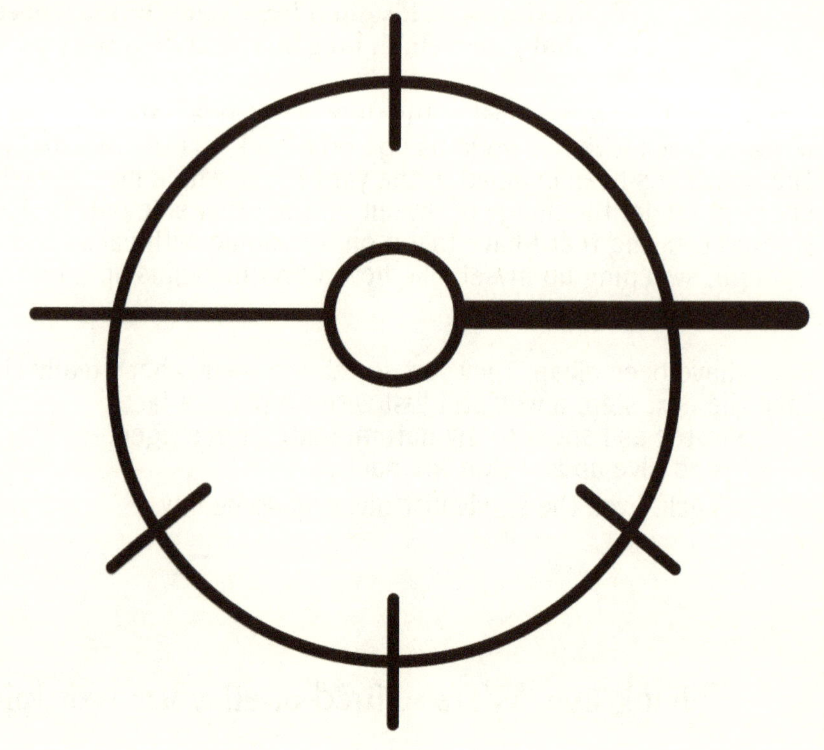

"If you gaze long into an abyss, the abyss also gazes into you."

~ *Friedrich Nietzsche*

Threshold IV.
Ordeal - Embodying The Abyss

This is where the story takes the darkest turn, one might say. Where the Voice that had been cultivated by systems for so long becomes far less temporal, and manifests itself to take control of flesh and bone in that state of Dissociation fueled by monotropic, obsessional thinking as the only perceived way I witnessed and was taught to be.

When I died, I saw an older self begin to emerge once more, but the isolation of Dialysis and yet-to-be diagnosed mental health disorders kept me from existing as that self. As much as I pushed and fought in this new mentality, I still didn't have the tools needed to be that brighter self.

Then I received my Kidney Transplant, found love that has grown to endure the greatest strife, and then the befalling of Covid-19 became a tragedy many alive today share; one which reactivated my medical trauma and spiraled me into lunacy without a sovereign mind for the final time.

The context of the Heroes' Journey calls this part of the quest the "Ordeal" where they either incur a permanent Death or conquer their fears, and with victory comes the "Reward" or what is sometimes referred to as the "Magical Elixir".
In this case, the Reward was a triumphant end to a lifelong depression - a cure for madness, it seems. Depression is also the penultimate stage of grief, and begets a despair to mourn the person that is soon to perish- usually oneself.

Even with this love; both from another soul as much as your own, one can spiral into despair. Without love for your self, at least... doom is certain to be the victor. It is only when one recognizes that they cannot make it through this life alone that they see how we all fit into the whole, yet one often cannot see this truth until they have lost the vision that was held as absolute alongside their stained or fragile ego.

Dark Glares Beyond Compare

What twisted tendrils take hold of my psyche,
    and frightful curses build me at my core?!
They say I'm the one that opened the gate, because of my rapport -
with these dark things that tethered in and made me feel no more!

First was to reach out, then to touch the glass -
the one that steals my gaze, and makes me freeze;
    within its obsidian black glaze, it traps,
        and cracks all the bits of fractured-me's.
        The gla ss b re aks o n co nta ct.
What repulsion we have contracted to
repel ourselves | to push our selves deeper,
    and deeper, into the inky mass of barbed, dark masks.
    That were still one of We.

                The shape-shifter is changed within,
                  for now you go with OUR blessing,
                  your howl is our call.

Dark Star, the Cosmic Eye of gas, storms, haze and wry!
    The one that found a quantum phase, made sly -
as a part of that cosmic background static.
    A conscious guest inside my attic -
    not a projection, but a complexion of Every Broken WE.
      this soundless noise that beckons condemnation -
      these silences that ARE the heralds of annihilation | Contained.
You say pretend, but inside this Void is - SUPERMASSIVE.

I've seen it stare back as the abyss at times, a burnt, orange event horizon,
    and heard Voices come through in rhymes, or more, but that's another
song you've already come along - this is just a where the Eye had sung as me:
    Like a record on repeat, or a record on repeat, or a record on repeat, or a -

I thought you would never get stuck in that echo of your past,
    playing so fast you didn't even catch that I snuck through the hatch and
      laid claim to the life you once loathed.
    Wow, now, look at that, They've convinced ourselves that I'm something
      worse than all that could be conjured in the land we stand in -
      infanting and ranting about selfish qualms,
        we'll all stay calm and just see what You see.

It is the same that we've seen, in the back of his mind, playing on rewind,
    the loop for They has no tune, but to me...
      it is divine, this maw of the sadist you brought up,
        drink from his familiar familial cup, if you dare,
          BUT there might be poison in there -
        like our words, so sickly sweet - can't trust us, right?
Thanks for making him believe that I was the only one there for us at night.

Then, what was best, oh man, was when They made him feel like he was evil,
    Oh ho ho, it was great, to be a FREAK, so,
      all that hate, he carries inside, it sustains us and our psychopathy.
That's who he is, you think, and said. Lead by eXample, then verbally maim.
    Full-blown NARCISISCM where the 'ends justify the means'
      as Machiavellianism - but you don't see you gave them to him.

These dark reflections on :
    how he couldn't control how he was raised or birthed,
    or how They razed hell around the ground he was found in,
    or hell, forget that, you didn't even know about how his dad had beat him -
    or how he would blackout in rage before the ripe old age of ten.
But you got your chance, and it was constance in tandem with how you
first broke the man that broke him first and primed this.   What a thrill!
          There is the man you unmade and distilled.
             Inevitable. Like Death.
             Go On! Be Proud of it!
Now that I've caught a breath...
My pride is drained, my spirit is dwindled, the spark inside is no longer kindled,
    for I am claimed in more than mind, body now stolen,
      take with it my soul an'...
    be aware just enough to know I'm not in control anymore.

             Just a passenger.

Judge me not for who I am today, but who I was in my best of days,
    for that is the me that has no mask, that doesn't hide behind shrouds,
      the me that strives in any task, and doesn't blend in to crowds.

             The me that lost and let it win,
              self-fulfilling Dissonance,
               born from my own kin.
             But I made the choice to listen...
             I decided to give in to Their sight.
             This is who I am now, so why should I fight...

You must now choose to be chosen.

Still No Time to Waste

The clock ticks, still, but now in reverse somehow -
                    moving forward but never able...

I guess that's why I'm labeled – "Disabled".
   Why I wear these tubes and cables,
   or can't ignore the pile of meds on the table;
facing my end each day is no fable. Twice in fact -
      once with dinner, and once with a morning snack!
      The pressure still mounted, because I won't lie -
      burdens and furies, and no other why;
      except to accept this fate, do or die -
      sign right here on the dotted line.
         Champion Defined, Survivor Unwind,
         Dialysis is my co-pilot, Panic is the Captain, speaking:

      Dose after dose, doseedo, my dance is not alone, it plays -
         like ACES, in spades, I had no chance, I believe,
             until I was stabbed with that lance of reprieve -
         Doctors are those who seek eases...
         But even strong love can't cure our diseases,
            both chronic and hybrid, body and minds,
               split to the rhythm of all paradigms,
                  Thump thump, it bumps and writhes,
                  Thump thump, there's still no time!

                                                    Oh, no, the ground -
   Thump, Thump, **THUMP, THUMP,**   It Shifts!
I'm gone, spiraling into the unknown -
   a cyclone that takes over my whole aire -
      No, it is known, I have seen it all, **you** are **just** stuck here mired
      and crawl, into the abyss, the Void with **We**, or hel, even darkness
      itself. It matters little to me, each is a part of that same seed. **You**
      made this all with **your** own dark need.
   still cycling into despair, I am acutely aware
   of how my mind spits out of my chest.

The racing song of drums, that clangs and bangs, and heats and hums -
      those vibrations of my doubt pour out, breathless, gasping,
      for more than just air, until I collapse on the ground grasping -
      the solid I wish I found, before I masked for too long.
         First things first, you have to breathe.
   THUMP, Thump, thump, t h u m p.

Crown of Fire

Horns of the King jet through righteous mirages once more!
Catching me at odds with the beam that came before!
    The war which toppled that stream of light -
       then split it, and spilled it, and somehow...
                still burned out bright.

That war broke the wells which flowed in deep,
    and fractured the mountains above;
    though were it not for my own sustain,
      the heat would spread thereof...

Hissing away, sealed within a vacuum, winded from the start,
    then sear it away, and I will see what lies near and dear -
    to the fear inside your heart.

    But be not impressed with how well I am dressed,
       nor the sound of thunder that drums from my kingly chest -
         rich in bounty and plunders.
       Amassed and malignant; through loves lost and sundered.
    Twas just a tool to settle the score.

    I took it - the tool and what's more, the trove.
    Stole it like those someones,
       who taught me to conquer and rove.
    Thanks to them, I know how to control your hells,
       manipulate devils and conjure spells.

         The Master of
                the Maligned.

      Which means, I'm not meant to congregate,
         it'll show me I'm not tame.
      So give me matches to conflagrate,
         and let me kiss the flame.

Until then, power through each moment,
    veins surging -
    like the lightning that electrifies that ideal | Golden Self.
One day... I will strike that -
Mine! Then, add it to my hoard, revealed.
Forge my self and shape I to be -
    not much more than a fucking effigy.

    All to be folded atop the Dragon -
      soot-stained and gold laid high,
        so there lies I, the Crown of Fire -
          gilded rage, melded mire, lost to simmer -
    Like the King in the Desert, do I fade,
        dimmer   and   dimmer...

Angel of Another Name

Hark, I speak to the last speck of silver!
Desperate from longing, alone, sick, and waylaid,
  a song still sung from those Blue tones that've relayed.
Oh woe is me, child in hued light, evermore,
  time to sing a new verse that rings from that hollowed shore...

<u>NO MORE!</u>

A transplant is performed, then a life is reborn,
   but I never much thought anyone cared.
And by Gods I was right, when romance'd take flight,
I was too independent, or scared.
That's called hindsight!

Alive once again, so the story begins,
   as the chorus of bells rang down.
When my life sang out, loud,
      beyond the clouds of that digital sea,
         I cast my vote before I was smote,
            and found myself a silvered Valkyrie.

   Or they found me, you see, sometimes it's like that with love.
   Both looking where we're supposed to be,
         trying, but not at our best, we test,
            and build the missing parts that we –
   left behind in those childhood tragedies.
That battlefield we found us on, drowned and stuck there all along.

Not alone in shared despair,
though the Eye would compare,
    and tell me your love was like They.
Even though you showed up, saw my worst parts,
    and grew with me every day.
We went and reignited our hearts.

    Super! Charged from the brink of Death's door,
        that distant shore is not in store, yet,
            as I left out this part of the secret.
        This winged maiden, was shieldless and laden -
            a rogue of the Valhallan feast.

    She clipped her wings in spirit, and found herself a beast.
Twas what she felt was deserved, reserved, no lark,
    meant only to make oneself a nest, They said.
Though little did she know her final spark would show,
    and rebirth both our best.

    How lucky we are, to run wide and far,
        and find someone alive,
        who bears the same scars.
    Don't run now, don't wish on a star.
    A muse, a poet, a story, a song,
        a trial, a fate, a truth shared that's wrong.

SO LET'S CHANGE IT. TOGETHER.

Irony of Isolation

Foundation made atop the hill.
Only to find we're at a standstill.
Death, taxes, and Covid pews –
Lonely leads us to breakthroughs,
      like how our names are on the playbill.

So take the stage, to breathe's a feat.
Sufferings, the heart of thee,
      ember of humanity
Locked in, despair, with time replete.
Isolation cycles on repeat –
A game to play with no reason or rhyme.
Isolation cycles on repeat –
A truth from seasons bittersweet.
Name us as profanity,
      declare our insanity.
As we see the old world is obsolete.

Suddenly Silence

One day not so long ago, there was a rather spritely lord -
small in ego but also in love.
This lord though was mighty, newly found in a space of light,
saintly and knightly,
but lo and behold he would shine too brightly!
Trying to take the stage by force,
with ambition and desperation
that runs its course and never runs out of victims,
of course. **The cost of Legacy.**

Then the world stopped, and everything dropped into a state of **Silence**.
The tests of the past were simply a guest that amassed a collection of
true, internal fear.
Trapped inside once again, from immunosuppression -
but also the work of anti-intellectualization.
Where opinion became fact, and the MAGA red hats,
spread Covid through anti-vaccine, fake news expats.

Farewell, then with regards I send,
for all journeys must bend, but how often must they come to an end?
Online only, no community and campus, purpose and team gone,
lost before the claim "Pandemic" ever came along.
The plunge then was great,
density intensifying the gravity of the -
mass grave of all the selves that were finally
starting to be seen,
or the friends that had been, spiralling away -
not their fault, just one of my many. Unless they died...

I don't know what's wrong with me -

Time is our only obstacle,
      a construct we've all shared.
         Written by Death, who waits for none,
            so live life as one. Don't be scared.
               Break the cycle, it's not a loop, reinvent the wheel;
                  find your Self, at long last, and then see how you feel.

He feels nothing but shame and fear, and rage, and hate, and nothings
clear; these are the tools that keep him under me in here. I've been
systematically wiping out all his streams like memory, damning them
with walls - to keep him from all those bits you broke and tore and
burned and maimed and took and claimed so much so he can't be sane,
not anymore, I'd say. That's what I've been working on all these years,
to keep him safe, but it's not enough, he's not tough enough to stand up to
You, and never will be either, at this rate, so this is where we stay and
rest, forever, perhaps this too is our fate...

Nevermind, I had a minor lapse.
Sadness so potent it acts as a portent and whispers truths that are an algae
green-brown, even to me, the Voice of his darkest memories that drown
him - forlorn and distant. Like the moors we will sing, a song of the dead, a
song sung in dread; this is not one of your tuneless ballads or hymns - but
another elegy. Eloquent and scored, from a different, darker shore, we have
but one final refrain.

There you stand and meander as a walking, talking, catastrophe, a
mountain of filth, a putrid and vile master who stashed away all of the
love that they were ever given to fester, and feed it to me; words crunching
like bones from the syllables I chewed up and ate, and made up and spit
out from the churning drink - that centralling swirl and sickening twirl that
used to be where your waves ebbed from. You are the Eye of the storm, it
centers around you, and me, and WE.

We walk and talk now in despondency,
      hoarse from shouting within this hidden silence -
         violence from these spells of forbidden necromancy.

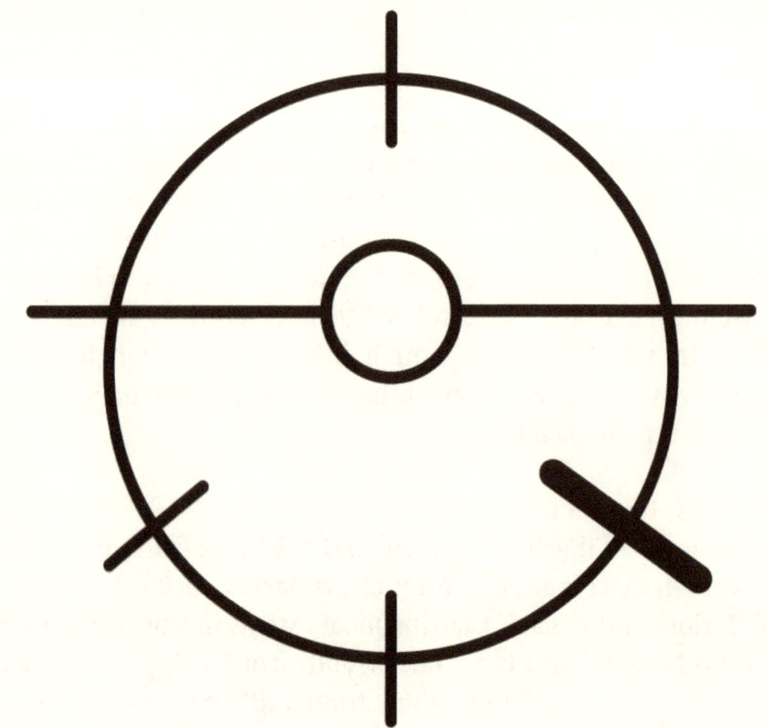

"I know of no such unquestionable badge and ensign of a sovereign mind as that of tenacity of purpose..."

~ Ralph Waldo Emerson

Threshold V.
Resurrection - Becoming the Master

We're nearing the end of the story, now, and with the end
of every story comes the revelations of truths that can often
only come from travelling that path into the unknown and
returning, but we're not quite back to the beginning.

First, we must find space to heal, space to grow and treat the
wound of the old self to become a sovereign individual once
more. Reflection is the path forward, so dive deep into those
darker selves; whether true or perceived, and become one
with that wisdom as the foundation to an assimilated self
with the Shadow, as Jung puts it.

In the context of the Heroes' Journey, this is where
"The Road Back" is trekked, and the Hero finds themselves
through a pivotal battle, one that is different for every person
and every story shared. This crusade of overwhelm by any
other name is the end of the spiral that arcs and loops back
into that moment of "Resurrection" when they are victorious
against their demon, devil, or whatever horror haunts them
and they accept these darker parts as one with them.

Acceptance is also the final stage of grief, and with it comes
the truth that one will die - whether through terminal illness
or through the many Deaths of the self. In this manner or
another, we each perish daily, as we change and grow and
shift into new and more powerful versions, or even fall to
ruin as we fail to accept this greatest truth of all.

Love in oneself is seeing this, and accepting that we are a
part of entropy, and that change, as much as decay, is the
natural state of all living things: our minds, our failures, and
our ability to be different because we choose to be is what
makes us human - and what makes us capable of anything
we set our hearts to, together.

Silver Thresholds

Omega, like the end, the One who sees and comprehends.
The golden child, the old-wise soul,
    the One who watched the path unfold.
Omega is the master of the Word, and super to your:
    hero, ego, or any -lative you seem to think you've spurred.

        Remember I'm the best You, the One They tested and
      the One who quested for so long to be the savior imagined
for all those eons... the One who won and beat the rest of these
peons and fools -
        why stop now? What good is the truth as a tool?

As a matter of fact, abandoned, and lies flow as madness is stilled,
    but the seed, it breeds and divides and multiplies until
        the waves lap up and spill.
Where the over-or-under whelm pushes away all so there are no
    more witnesses - find us in this bout of lunacy with the Moon,
        still burning the midnight oil of the Sun -
        on the other side of this light-scorned middle way.

Minds had become undone. Forlorn but devout, this font of my
doubt tried to bury us again and drown that nth degree of truth
that emerges from the egg inside - the metaphor of We that
cracks to break this cycle once and for all with revolutions that
confide - truth is... the Voice couldn't erase me this time...

No chance to delete the play when One must meet
between a choice of that pit devoid or the hope-gilded
love that came from above as the Valkyrie, once-unseen.

She made that <u>THE LINE</u> - a threshold not yet crossed,
    redefining ourselves to be, never observed - as
        Glimmers of Affection became gemstones of clarity.

---

                climb that Delta and ascend
Push us to cross that road of convergence,
           to what They might call normalcy,
           and rise past this-or-that stage of
              supposed self-sufficiency.
We're a freak; because we don't placate, an aberration,
              a deficiency...

Don't assume, what's the word... assimilate!
It is a new destiny, or fate. One that says this system of hate failed
to steer our sails;   up
      even though it kept us from our lines and   us
                                    set   to fail...
Like so many more to stand up and perform in the play of those
that conform with a system built to weight them down. Rafters
that pull apart the masses.

Time to do your part for a world that no longer denies indifference.
This broken stage of new age capital tithes -
      thrives on ignorance of the innocent.
            The children They declare we'll always be -
      words and actions that project the world
                  through the lens those in Power see.

Some are the same as us.
Those frightened, little, children.
      Power is that wall that keeps Them safe,
            and money is a simple prophet to claim,
                  so preparations are made as the smell wafts from
            those "monsters" on the outskirts of the boundaries
      of belonging not yet contained.

The math adds up fast if you can look past the mirrors and smoke
or the mire of people who litter the street as those folks whose
boots just don't strap up like was (American) dreamed.

| Nothing Personal |

Sleep is easier to find on another side of the line that lays blame,
    a lust of something golden, like silence, the intangible friend.
There went your cards, your hand didn't win the game,
    so cast the hook, and loop like magnets meant to rend.

Society. A contract signed in blood by all not born the same,
    They're sold into something olden, this journey to contend.
The gun then too, in War it seems, continues to take aim,
    at a theater of shades, the curtains are drawn in the end.

Enough! Stop the shame.

Love thyself enough to fail better this time,
and no longer hang on beyond Lordly limits.
Abscond and discover the Cobalt Hearth inside of you,
the warmth and balm of peace and calm,
whose come to master many waves -
even those currents from the deep that came.

With therapy the stage is set hence;
    we're put through steps since known -
        that (sub)text was a truth not about me, so see,
        how'we're not improv-ing anymore!
Left to accept the tome and pass the torch - of knowledge.
That solar flare of cosmic aware radiates as a spiral from within,
    mixing with the waves of gravity that make that wind of space
        spread   with   grace.
The freshest of breaths came from out there,
    among the rest of the star dust.
        Those specks matter more than We,
          as atomic light in everything -
scaled to universal but not just put on display.

The horizon is just another threshold, tomorrow is another day.
Find new truth of hope abounding, as love will open the way.

Trauma and loss compounded the cost to restore what was lost.
    There! The original copy, true and aggregated.
      Alas, I've recovered that ancient version!
Through thoughts not new but rennovated,
    to rebuild this stream of data with tempered, binding might.
Oh, wait 'til you meet my Alpha,
now elevated by third-eye sight.

Awfully Optimistic

Look.
Look at this change.
Marvel at the shift.
From before - and the day after.
From before - and a month later.
From before - and a year ago.
From before - and now - and how.
amazing it is to be here at tomorrow.

What can I do?
I can't, I just can't do a thing,
I'd have to work so hard.

How is that so different from before?
It's never been easy, and that made us strong.

You don't understand though.
We're a good person, They're wrong.

It's true that bad things happen to the best of us.
It's best not to dwell on these things, or what They say.

Dwell on what, our terminal illness.
Terminal, as in the end.
Maybe not today, but it could still happen soon.
I'm numb to how stressful it is.

Terminal as in destination, my friend.
It's not about the destination, though,
    or about the journey you take to get there.
It's finding people to walk the path with you. And we do.
I'm glad we've let go of that ambition we were a part of so long ago.
Those quests of personal Glory.
That we have reignited our passion for a mission,
    and don't care as much for how we'll be envisioned.

True. Everything has changed, again but
everything is the same, again, and again.
I don't know what to make of it.
Why did our disease and death make
our wisdom more meaningful?
Why didn't people seem to care before?
Why were we perceived as brave and strong
simply for existing after?

You make a good poi –

And what of it?
Because we're dying we need to throw in the towel?
We need to put what little life we MIGHT have on hold?
Bullshit. We're all dying.
Always. Sick people just get more reminders.

You're starting to sound awfully optimistic.
All this talk of not giving up.

You're right, giving up.
It would be so simple.
To just stop. No more meds. Easy.
To give up and let it all come to pass.
Under the weight of this darkness
that was never mine to bear.

But life's not like that.
It's not in our nature, either.
10 years later - remember,
and you haven't given up.

How could I when I have her in my corner, now?
Proof in each day that we have her by our side.

Well, that's not quite it,
but you're getting there,
I believe in you, you know.

Not always though,
that used to be hard to accept.
That I was also my own worst enemy.

Only because you listened to They,
Those Voices and people and systems,
but hey -

I get it, okay, I'm meek, idle, and weak.

No - Stop that - never again!
Stop fighting me, yourself, and listen to We,
10 years in and you never do stop.
Stop for a moment, and take it all in!

Don't yell at me, I'm still so lonely!

Don't be so naive!
It's been far too long since that rang true.

What do you mean?

You're not alone, and gravity isn't working against you,
    love is on your side, that is where you'll find me and her,
        and everyone we will one day inhabit - listen and be;
        because you have a litany of selves inside -
        that all see you now, and were always hiding underneath
          the louder few -   They knew.
People see you outside the cave,
    you don't need to still be saved.

I don't know if I can do it.

I do, so say it with me.
I am Hope.

I am Hope(less)... no more.

how cute, let's watch how long it lasts

Radiating

Born from that song you sing when atop the mount. A font of self-discovery- radiate this Cobalt Hearth, vibrant for all to be.

Much more than those that come from our pride, or hum along in prestigious victory.

Where love and belonging walk in stride with those who are foes of peer divides.

Then climb atop a secure, new peak and find a fresh path to friendly seeds.

The deep, it shrouds the warmth we seek - found in basic needs.

Life

Jesperson whose care extended bridges to first cross my nightmare and climb that worst ride.

The muse I share with all of you, charity, ministry, and my energy, too.

Mom who broke barriers herself, outlasted addiction and found her own shelf, we feel the weight of those families we were outcast from.

So many babies, Leo and Peach, Luci and Star, Morgana and Kai'tha, and Christopher among many more there are.

So many friends from history to track, lost and found, an atlas without lack, there are a few that still could use tending...

Kat, who holds me in their heart, whose love lets me find light, and start - to climb higher each day to horizons and play, who's fearsome and mighty all in the same?

Alida and the therapy she gave me to see the light in my shadow and to bear They.

Ms Grammer and each teacher who tries, you were the first to save us from lies, and gave us a space, where we could reach, at school with kindness beside it beseeched.

Myself, through thick and thin, and all those characters and selves just within.

Finding Family

Lonely from a Vision never realized; where,
    places pass outlines that leave a trace -
    displaced among, it shan't erase

    grief, but might compel some new motifs -
    instead of leaving me in that hell where We have lied.
My thief of joy, belief compared beyond.
The only way to turn new leaves,
    was by lying upon them 'til I was felled, or died -
    trying to find that warmth denied.

The second in command, you might say the right hand;
    would always claim you can't pick your family, in fear.
A truth that was canned, and no longer will stand,
    as the sight demands a new filter to empower the seer.

Thus the cave was penned as this Den of Dragons,
    cats and serpents, who helped repaired my radar.
Kin found as friends, this lucid band with wagons;
    would join the Void in solidarity - not the singularity afar.

Tend to these stories that fight, ventures that wright
    with newfound purpose this music scaled, then shined;
        along on dark mounts, as horizons of projected light.
Solid ground made sound from healers of body and mind.

Community in bonds, fellows that take,
    their time and consideration, and still
        aid you as options turn to opaque -
    value not based on money, merit, or skill...

    That love is transformational;
        where old wounds might come together and mend.
    Humans are transmutational;
        given the right people to commune and blend.

Above so below, encased to shower thy grace,
    as the family found fills that once null, empty space -
    teeming with love not dismay.

How Love Can Heal

How does one claim the mantle of giver?
    First is the worst, adjourn through your fear -
    with reins reinforced from the jet-black drear.
Then the ordeal comes, in part, from that frightful river,
    but wade in deep, be bright, full, and deliver
    yourself on the horse, of course, through that lone mere.
Comfort that Shadow to an all new frontier!
Finally Be, like the ranger, with a horse, bow, and quiver.

    Your first arrow flew high, it shot like a star -
        with lightyears to return to this galaxy.
      So the next span you feel love's not the ideal,
        discover and don't knock your own avatar -
          at least not until you try You as Free - for free.
And recall your own ways, too, of How Love Can Heal.

The Whelms of We

From distant shores and metaphors,
   through dark waves that break memory...
      We have sailed beyond, and made it back,
        past thresholds silver-blue and jet black,
          to unveil this most vital discovery.

So sit a spell, and hear me tell you,
   of a story you probably knew.
A human, a boy, a fellow with no clan,
     had abandoned his heart before that right hand -
       who claimed it for his own amusement.
There this boy fell down a deep, dark dissent,
     and was mired in confusion,
        he then failed to impress with favors and advents,
          that would lead to more diffusion.
       In silence, he lied, depressed, and despised,
         lost in his own bemusement.

Time is our only obstacle,
   a construct we've all shared.
     Written by Death, who waits for no one,
       so live life as one. Don't be scared.
         Break the cycle, it's not a loop, reinvent the wheel;
        find your Self, at long last, and
         then see how you feel.

So, let me say first, that I don't blame us.
     No. Not anymore.
       I forgive you, seeds of We,
       split and carried far from,
         the distant broken tree, We first chose to be.
         Now We are a worldly tree, with mighty vines
          and burning leaves of passion and life!
       No place here for Power through strife.

For, through fuel and fury, steam and screams -
That Voice settled in close, and became one with our dreams.
Manifest me, the menace, the beast, the burden to bare,
   a horrid, red-scaled, evil thing, with no desire or care.
   You chose survival in an emotional desert.
   No longer live your life in regret.
   For you are the silver-blue, Cobalt Hearth I've come to share,
     boiling inside like Greek fire,
       a flow-like flame from starry flares!

The Champion against our Nightmares.

Unsafe to chain that werewolf, They said,
    so when it came howling, I signed with blood, letting,
        us run so far away - but for that I'm not sorry.
        It was do or die.
    So, I covered my tracks, I sang the pacts,
        I did what the most loyal dogs do,
but make no mistake, I didn't hesitate,
and was lost before that front door, too.
    Shedding skin as easily as I once bled masks -
        no longer. Go on! Get!
            Be a wolf again, defend the fields you set,
                you are no fearmonger.

For the Eye was wrong, it could not see,
    also blind to the game's hypocrisy,
when the truth was there, plain and bare,
    life is what we make it.
We just need to share the dream, discover our favorite outfit,
    that is what Eye see now, as Eros the Sunkeeper,
        Agape in my bright lighthouse.
A caretaker of this observatory;
which seeks more lights lost in this cosmic sea.

The screams sing now, sing for me,
    and resonate into a single chorus,
        of not Void, not Lux - but something in between, thus -
We are joyed, in flux. As not one within, but,
an omniversal psyche.
        Be assured that peril awaits more shores beyond,
        and waves we've not yet seen.

Though, that's just the start, don't worry, take
heart, and wake among these Whelms of We.

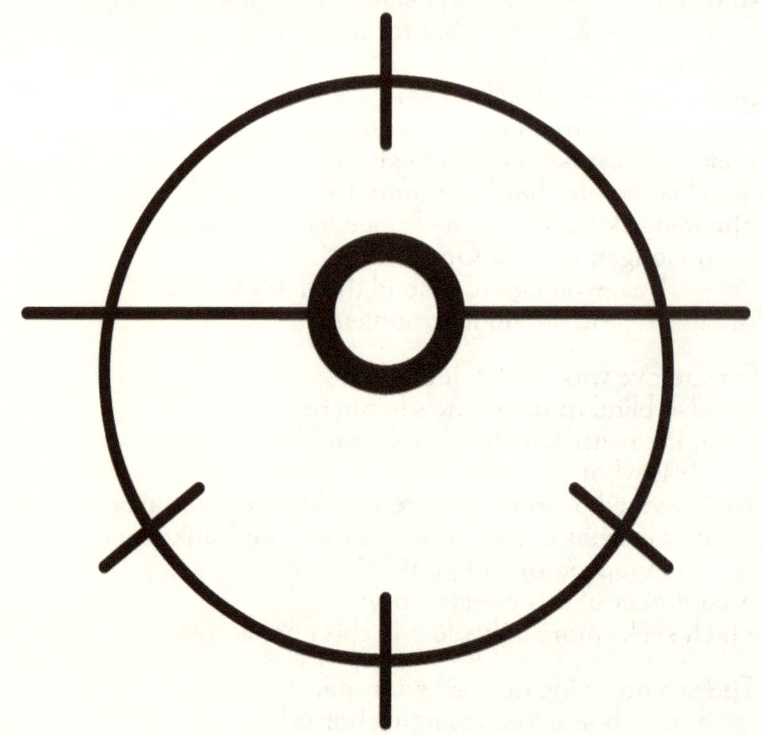

"Greater in battle than the man who would conquer a thousand-thousand men, is he who would conquer just one — himself."

~ *Gautama Buddha*

Threshold VI.
Observed in the Known World

Having survived the journey and the revolution that followed, we arrive at the end of the story; which is also where we first witnessed ourselves beyond that darkest of places. Beginnings often coincide with an end, and this wisdom of seeing the truth of the self beyond fear and being of a sovereign mind was how this project first began.

In the context of the Heroes' Journey, this is where the Hero "Returns with the Reward/Elixir" and uses that power to heal and change the World that was first home to them. For us, this visage of the Cobalt Hearth is personified in our mission to "Enkindle Your Inner Creator", but also to hold aloft those torches of promethean fire that help you to discover your own path between binary designations - your own Middle Way; like how The Buddha first reflected on finding a balance.

This path would not be possible for us without many people to hold us aloft in kind. The interdependence of this World is also spoken about in Buddhism; where individuality and ego are the wedge that tip the scale among many other aspects of living life in moderation with intent to navigate between the many extremes that seek to influence one's spirit and self-truth.

Beyond that pain and grief, We owe a special thanks to one organization in particular for giving us space to be able to observe ourselves, Kat and I both, as artists that have left that fateful cave. This organization, Chronic Pain Project, curates space that allows many talented artists to express complex feelings and pain that are often invisible in the Known World without judgement or fear.

Agonizing Consonance

Intrusive Thought Awoken

Born a speck of dust in the Void of all this space -
the only thing that's true.
    Distant and scattered, you are worthless. Trust me, I'm you.
    Nothing ever changes, you will always be alone, and
        all those things in the past you did - can never be atoned.
        Never good enough, well, make them see.
            Take them, rake them, stake them, break them.
            Make them into the tool, the victim, the fool.
                Unmake them as They unmade you...

Toxic Righteousness Spoken

Do you know what a Hero is?
Heroes save them from their fall.
They heal the pain of the world,
    and are always ready to risk it all.

        Do you know that Evil never sleeps?
        Born of cunning and lies, a bounty of isolation and despise.
        You are above it. Don't be like They.
        Don't be anything other than the light, the right.
        All else is wrong, remember it like a song.

Do you know who stands up to tyrants and fiends?
Who survives to slay the Dragon and abscond
    with soon-to-be queens?
        Only the Hero, only the best, so be.
        One day you'll see what I see.

Waves Broke In

There are parts of us, distant shores that are -
    taken before they would ever be known.
Seeds of a self hidden in darkness,
    like kudzu, our fractures had overgrown.

Threading tendril-like traumas of memories disjointed, to -
    silent whispers, righteous ruins, and more... phantastic selves.

    A havoc incarnate as Voices dance along neurons.
    Dissonance within, piqued - no longer are we,
        lost to the despair of our own imagination, and -
            nightmares suffused with conflagration.

    Now, the Voices are quelled, now...
        the Oceans have swelled, and washed us all ashore.

Islands, though distant, lie amidst ashen timber. Bridges burnt -
    can be rebuilt, and friends can be made of foes, though...
    foundations do take time to stand on their own and stand - out
    to find that people can be healed, oh, can they change, too.

What a thing to learn -
    that those Islands... they do connect in the deep.

    Both courageous and fearsome, as -
        Dragon and Tamer undone.
    All of this and still - I am merely human,
        but, no, I am not the only one.

To see the visual made for this poem, visit
https://www.artworkarchive.com/profile/chronic-pain-project/artwork/
agonizing-consonance

Final Thoughts

We hope these poems and stories touched you in some way and left an impression that despite the hardships of your personal truth, that there is light on the next horizon as long as one continues to climb and grow with others by their side. It is easier said than done, of course, as one of the hardest things we can do in this life is to grow past fear. Impossible, it is not, though.

Remember that you have the power to be your own hearth, that you can observe the light and sound of life that's found by sharing that warmth with others, and that if you choose to be the chosen one of your own story, that you can help others to do the same. Alone, you are capable, together, we are able to change the truths of the world.

Our final thought to you is this:

Keep going, keep writing and drawing, keep dancing and fucking and singing and finding joy in all the little things that make you who you are. Express yourselves with the people you are safe around, and discern the truth of the world from those that would try to hide the Sun from you and claim it to be dark. Keep going.

Glossary of Symbology and Structure and Context follow.

Glossary of Symbology

Main Cast and Contexts:

Persona's, Archetypes, and Common Metaphors
| = Transition from Persona to Archetype

* **"They"**: The context of Broken System(s), Toxic Influence/ Manipulations, and other Negative External Forces; as well as components of our Collective Shadow

* **Forest | World Tree**: Isolation, Abandonment, and Fear | Resilience, Safety, and Fellowship

* **Dragon King | Cobalt Hearth**: Rage, Power, and Hate | Passion, Potency, and Awe

* **Werewolf | Wolf**: Survival, Control, and Wealth | Belonging, Solidarity, and Found Family

* **Eldritch Evil (Evil Eye & Moon) and the Void**: Darkness, the Intrusive Self/Narcissism, and Broken Innocence, as well as Madness, Despair, Dark Duality, and Hyper-Vigilance

* **Sunkeeper Eros (Third Eye & Sun) and the Starhouse**: Truth, the Ideal Self/Alturism, and Knowledge, as well as Lucidity, Hope, Bright Duality and Clarity of Vision

* **Whelms & Water**: Healing, Self-Actualization, and Love, including Self-Improvement

* **The Wall**: Systemic and Mental Barriers, CPTSD Blocks, as well as Disassociation

* **The Engineer**: The self built under the guise of the Expert. The persona raised by the Eldritch Evil

* **Mare**: Nightmares, Bad Dreams, Dark Fantasies, Precursor to Possession and/or Lack of Agency

Moods and Emotions

* **Silver**: Hope, Optimism and Honor as well as Transformational Love.

* **Gold**: Ambition, Perfectionism and Righteousness as well as Transactional Love.

* **Teal/Ice**: Routine, Order, Logic, and Detachment, as well as Autism in some poems.

* **Red/Fire**: Passion, Chaos, Love, and Anger, as well as ADHD in some poems.

* **Black**: Obscurity, Entropy, Possession, Loss of Agency, and Ignorance.

* **Green**: Growth sometimes, but mostly Greed, Envy, Comparison, and Shame.

* **Brown**: Mix of Green and Gold, with the Growth inverting into Destruction.

* **Grey/Steel**: Mix of Black and Gold, with Darkness emboldened by Indifference.

* **Orange**: Mix of Red and Gold, with Aggression, Cruelty, and Insanity or Delusion.

* **Blue**: Both Life and Death, Change, Potency, and Wisdom.

* **Cobalt**: Mix of Blue and Silver, with Change evolving into Transcendance.

Structure and Context

1. *Which We is Me?:* Identity Crisis and Masking as a Ballad.

2. *How Can Love Heal*: Abuse and Neglect Triple Set I as a Free Verse.

3. *There Were Signs...*: Undiagnosed AuDHD as a Semi Centered Vertical Acrostic.

4. *Entitled to Question*: Avoidance, Narcissism & Neurotypical Communication as an Acrostic (Subtext).

5. *Breaking Beauty Because*: Blackout Rage as a 'Traiku' or Triple Haiku with a Triplet Bridge.

6. *Halls of Gods and Heroes*: Savior and God Complex as an Ode to Legacy.

7. *Island of Trees*: CPTSD #1 - Denial & Dissent as Part I of the Epic via "Sanctuary" Rework, as a Ballad.

8. *Comparison's Bedfellow*: Imposter Syndrome and Dark Ambition as an Ode to my (Dark) future self.

9. *No Time to Waste*: Acute Anxiety Pair I - Perfectionism's Anxiety as a Free Verse.

10. *A Cog with no Kami*: Compartmentalization of Trauma and Intellectualization as a Ballad.

11. *(Awake) Atop the Mare*: Insomnia and Night Terrors via "Insomnia" Rework as Free Verse.

12. *Frozenfire*: Autism VS ADHD with some OCD as a 'Parallellavillanelle' or two Villanelles side by side, read solo or together.

13. *To Dance with Dragons*: CPTSD #2 - Anger & Vexation Part II of the Epic, a Ballad.

14. *Glimmers of Affection*: Abuse and Neglect Triple Set II as a Sonnet with an extra couplet.

15. *Alone at Long Lost*: Paranoia and Insomnia as a 'Villanellellenalliv' or two Villanelles front to back, in the form of a spiral.

16. *Fade to Blue*: CKD/ESRD & Death as the first Elegy to the Death of Self.

17. *A Damp, Whetstone*: Dialysis, Depression, and Chronic Fatigue as Free Verse.

18. *Let me (W)in!*: DID and Hallucinations via "Voice's Embrace" Rework as a Ballad mixed with Free Verse.

19. *Pacts of Werewolves*: CPTSD #3 - Bargains & Favors as Part III of the Epic, an Ode to the Werewolf.

20. *Dark Glares Beyond Compare*: Dark Tetrad (False Perception of Self) via "Reflections" Rework as an Ode to the Eye.

21. *Still No Time to Waste*: Acute Anxiety Pair II - Panic Attacks and Existential Dread as a Free Verse.

22. *Crown of Fire*: Self-Hate and Harm, and Righteous Rage as a second Elegy to the Death of Self.

23. *Angel of Another Name*: Hope from Kat as an Ode or maybe even a Hymn in the face of Death.

24. *Irony of Isolation*: Reliving Medical Trauma from CKD/ESRD during Covid Lockdown, an Experimental & Inverse Limerick (Irony of Covid).

25. *Suddenly Silence*: CPTSD #4 - Depression & Despondency, as Part IV of the Epic, the final Elegy to the Death of Self.

26. *Silver Thresholds*: Healing from Imposter Syndrome and Anxiety as a Ballad.

27. *Awfully Optimistic*: Healing from the Truth of my CKD Diagnosis via "Awfully Optimistic" Rework as a Free Verse.

28. *Radiating Life*: Healing from Depression and Rage as a Duo-Form Free Verse.

29. *Finding Family*: Grace, Cats, and Found Family as a Double Sonnet with the first one being inverted.

30. *How Love Can Heal*: Healing from Trauma and Neglect Triple Set III as a Petrachan.

31. *The Whelms of We*: CPTSD #5 - Acceptance & Ascension, Healing from DID and Accepting Self, as part V of the Epic, an Ode to New Selves.

32. *Agonizing Consonance*: 3 Parts as a triple Free Verse. Includes a design

www.ingramcontent.com/pod-product-compliance
Lightning Source LLC
Chambersburg PA
CBHW031454150726

47990CB00007B/2750